THIS BOOK BELONGS TO

....

WELCOME!

A QUICK INTRODUCTION ON HOW TO USE THIS BOOK:

DECLUTTER YOUR MIND FIRST BY SETTING CLEAR GOALS BEFORE GETTING GOING. YOU DON'T WANT TO END UP WITH BIGGER MESS THAN THE ONE YOU STARTED WITH!

USE THE GIVEN LIST OF FEW EXAMPLES OF 15-MINUTE SPEED ACTION CLEANING TO HELP WITH YOUR WEEKLY AND MONTHLY PLANNING.
USE THE 30 DAY CHALLENGES TO ORGANIZE THE TIME AND ACTIONS YOU INTEND TO MAKE TO ACHIEVE YOUR GOAL EACH MONTH.

ROUTINES WORK BEST. MAKE A ROUTINE FOR YOURSELF ON WEEKLY BASIS FOR DIFFERENT AREAS IN YOUR HOME, AND TRY STICKING TO IT.
DIVIDE YOUR MONTHLY CLEANING CHORES INTO SMALLER, WEEKLY TASKS SO YOU WON'T FEEL OVERWHELMED WHEN YOU SEE THE BIGGER PICTURE SECTIONED INTO SMALLER PIECES.

WRITE WHAT WILL YOU DO WITH THE ITEMS YOU DECIDED YOU NO LONGER NEED.
WILL YOU GIVE THEM AWAY, SELL THEM, OR JUST THROW THEM OUT?

TAKE NOTES FOR EVERYTHING YOU FEEL NECESSARY IN THE SPACE PROVIDED.

ENJOY YOUR RENEWED HOME!

DECLUTTER YOUR MIND FIRST

SET YOUR TEN DECLUTTERING GOALS.
CHECK OFF AS YOU COMPLETE EACH ONE.

1. ☐
2. ☐
3. ☐
4. ☐
5. ☐
6. ☐
7. ☐
8. ☐
9. ☐
10. ☐

SIX STEPS & PRINCIPLES TO FOLLOW

1. IMAGINE VIVIDLY ON HOW DO YOU WANT YOUR HOME TO LOOK AND FEEL.

2. PUT ALL THE ITEMS FROM A PARTICULAR CATEGORY, NOT ROOM, IN A PILE.

3. TOUCH AND FEEL EVERY ITEM FROM THE PILE. ASK YOURSELF: DOES THIS PARTICULAR ITEM BRINGS ME JOY?

4. IF AN ITEM DOESN'T INSPIRE THAT FEELING, THANK IT FOR ITS SERVICE SO FAR, AND THINK IF YOU SHOULD GIVE IT AWAY, SELL IT OR THROW IT AWAY.

5. HAVE OR MAKE ROOM FOR EVERYTHING.

6. PLACE THE ITEMS UPRIGHT WHEN ORGANIZING, TO MAKE SURE THEY ARE VISIBLE

GOAL NO.1

AFTERWARDS MY HOUSE WILL LOOK LIKE:

PLACES TO LOOK FOR INSPIRATION:

BREAK IT DOWN

STEP 1

STEP 2

STEP 3

STEP 4

SHOPPING LIST

GOAL NO.2

AFTERWARDS MY HOUSE WILL LOOK LIKE:

PLACES TO LOOK FOR INSPIRATION:

BREAK IT DOWN

STEP 1

STEP 2

STEP 3

STEP 4

SHOPPING LIST

GOAL NO.3

AFTERWARDS MY HOUSE WILL LOOK LIKE:

....

....

PLACES TO LOOK FOR INSPIRATION:

....

....

BREAK IT DOWN

STEP 1	STEP 2
STEP 3	STEP 4

SHOPPING LIST

....	....
....	....
....	....
....	....

GOAL NO.4

AFTERWARDS MY HOUSE WILL LOOK LIKE:

....

....

PLACES TO LOOK FOR INSPIRATION:

....

....

BREAK IT DOWN

STEP 1	STEP 2
STEP 3	STEP 4

SHOPPING LIST

....	....
....	....
....	....
....	....

GOAL NO.5

AFTERWARDS MY HOUSE WILL LOOK LIKE:

....

....

PLACES TO LOOK FOR INSPIRATION:

....

....

BREAK IT DOWN

STEP 1	STEP 2
STEP 3	STEP 4

SHOPPING LIST

....	....
....	....
....	....
....	....

GOAL NO.6

AFTERWARDS MY HOUSE WILL LOOK LIKE:

PLACES TO LOOK FOR INSPIRATION:

BREAK IT DOWN

STEP 1

STEP 2

STEP 3

STEP 4

SHOPPING LIST

GOAL NO.7

AFTERWARDS MY HOUSE WILL LOOK LIKE:

....

....

PLACES TO LOOK FOR INSPIRATION:

....

....

BREAK IT DOWN

STEP 1	STEP 2
STEP 3	STEP 4

SHOPPING LIST

....	....
....	....
....	....
....	....

GOAL NO.8

AFTERWARDS MY HOUSE WILL LOOK LIKE:

....

....

PLACES TO LOOK FOR INSPIRATION:

....

BREAK IT DOWN

STEP 1	STEP 2
STEP 3	STEP 4

SHOPPING LIST

....	....
....	....
....	....
....	....

GOAL NO.9

AFTERWARDS MY HOUSE WILL LOOK LIKE:

....

....

PLACES TO LOOK FOR INSPIRATION:

....

....

BREAK IT DOWN

STEP 1	STEP 2
STEP 3	STEP 4

SHOPPING LIST

....	....
....	....
....	....
....	....

GOAL NO. 10

AFTERWARDS MY HOUSE WILL LOOK LIKE:

....

....

PLACES TO LOOK FOR INSPIRATION:

....

....

BREAK IT DOWN

STEP 1	STEP 2
STEP 3	STEP 4

SHOPPING LIST

....

....

....

....

15 MINUTE CLUTTER BUSTERS
AND SPACE FOR YOUR OWN

THROW AWAY EXPIRED FOOD & MEDICINE

CHANGE SHEETS AND MAKE THE BED

WASH THE BATHROOM FLOORS

EMPTY THE DISHWASHER

CLEAN THE MIRRORS

WASH OUT LUNCHBOXES

EMPTY THE GARBAGE CAN

VACUUM A ROOM

CLEAN OUT THE MICROWAVE

SORT AND START A LOAD OF LAUNDRY

WIPE DOWN THE FRONT DOOR

WIPE DOWN THE DOORKNOBS

SCRUB THE KITCHEN SINK

SORT OUT THE MAIL

CLEAN THE BATHTUB OR THE SHOWER

WIPE OUT AND TIDY UP THE FRIDGE

FOLD A BASKET OF LAUNDRY

WASH THE KITCHEN FLOOR

PICK UP CLUTTER IN THE KITCHEN

30 DAY MONTHLY CHALLENGE

GOAL FOR THE MONTH:　　　　J F M A M J J A S O N D

M	T	W	T	F	S	S

NOTES

MONTHLY PLAN

CHORES TO COMPLETE

WEEK BY WEEK

WEEK 1

WEEK 2

WEEK 3

WEEK 4

CLEANING CHECKLIST

KITCHEN:

- EMPTY THE DISHWASHER
- CLEAN ALL THE SURFACES
- TAKE OUT THE TRASH
- CLEAN THE REFRIGERATOR
- CLEAN THE OVEN
- SWEEP AND MOP THE FLOOR
-
-

LIVING ROOM:

- VACUUM THE COUCH
- VACUUM THE FLOOR
- WIPE SURFACES
- ARRANGE THE COUCH PILLOW
- CLEAN THE TV
- CHANGE THE CURTAINS
-
-

BATHROOM:

- CLEAN THE BATHTUB
- CLEAN THE TOILET
- CHANGE & WASH TOWELS
- REPLENISH TOILETRIES
- REFILL TOILET PAPER
- MOP THE FLOOR
-
-

BEDROOMS:

- CHANGE THE BED COVERS
- SWEEP & MOP THE FLOOR
- WASH THE LINENS
- ARRANGE THE DRESSER
- DUST PILLOWS
- CLEAN ALL THE SURFACES
-
-

OTHER:

-
-
-
-
-
-
-

OTHER:

-
-
-
-
-
-
-

ITEMS TO LET GO

SELL

DONATE

THROW AWAY

REPAIR OR REPLACE

REPAIR

REPLACE

NOTES

NOTES

30 DAY MONTHLY CHALLENGE

GOAL FOR THE MONTH:　　　　　　　J F M A M J J A S O N D

M	T	W	T	F	S	S

NOTES

MONTHLY PLAN

CHORES TO COMPLETE

WEEK BY WEEK

WEEK 1

WEEK 2

WEEK 3

WEEK 4

CLEANING CHECKLIST

KITCHEN:

- EMPTY THE DISHWASHER
- CLEAN ALL THE SURFACES
- TAKE OUT THE TRASH
- CLEAN THE REFRIGERATOR
- CLEAN THE OVEN
- SWEEP AND MOP THE FLOOR

LIVING ROOM:

- VACUUM THE COUCH
- VACUUM THE FLOOR
- WIPE SURFACES
- ARRANGE THE COUCH PILLOW
- CLEAN THE TV
- CHANGE THE CURTAINS

BATHROOM:

- CLEAN THE BATHTUB
- CLEAN THE TOILET
- CHANGE & WASH TOWELS
- REPLENISH TOILETRIES
- REFILL TOILET PAPER
- MOP THE FLOOR

BEDROOMS:

- CHANGE THE BED COVERS
- SWEEP & MOP THE FLOOR
- WASH THE LINENS
- ARRANGE THE DRESSER
- DUST PILLOWS
- CLEAN ALL THE SURFACES

OTHER:

OTHER:

ITEMS TO LET GO

SELL

DONATE

THROW AWAY

REPAIR OR REPLACE

REPAIR

REPLACE

NOTES

NOTES

30 DAY MONTHLY CHALLENGE

GOAL FOR THE MONTH:　　　　　J F M A M J J A S O N D

M	T	W	T	F	S	S

NOTES

MONTHLY PLAN

CHORES TO COMPLETE

WEEK BY WEEK

WEEK 1

WEEK 2

WEEK 3

WEEK 4

CLEANING CHECKLIST

KITCHEN:

- EMPTY THE DISHWASHER
- CLEAN ALL THE SURFACES
- TAKE OUT THE TRASH
- CLEAN THE REFRIGERATOR
- CLEAN THE OVEN
- SWEEP AND MOP THE FLOOR
-
-

LIVING ROOM:

- VACUUM THE COUCH
- VACUUM THE FLOOR
- WIPE SURFACES
- ARRANGE THE COUCH PILLOW
- CLEAN THE TV
- CHANGE THE CURTAINS
-
-

BATHROOM:

- CLEAN THE BATHTUB
- CLEAN THE TOILET
- CHANGE & WASH TOWELS
- REPLENISH TOILETRIES
- REFILL TOILET PAPER
- MOP THE FLOOR
-
-

BEDROOMS:

- CHANGE THE BED COVERS
- SWEEP & MOP THE FLOOR
- WASH THE LINENS
- ARRANGE THE DRESSER
- DUST PILLOWS
- CLEAN ALL THE SURFACES
-
-

OTHER:

-
-
-
-
-
-
-
-

OTHER:

-
-
-
-
-
-
-
-

ITEMS TO LET GO

SELL

DONATE

THROW AWAY

REPAIR OR REPLACE

REPAIR

REPLACE

NOTES

NOTES

30 DAY MONTHLY CHALLENGE

GOAL FOR THE MONTH: J F M A M J J A S O N D

M	T	W	T	F	S	S

NOTES

MONTHLY PLAN

CHORES TO COMPLETE

WEEK BY WEEK

WEEK 1

WEEK 2

WEEK 3

WEEK 4

CLEANING CHECKLIST

KITCHEN:

- EMPTY THE DISHWASHER
- CLEAN ALL THE SURFACES
- TAKE OUT THE TRASH
- CLEAN THE REFRIGERATOR
- CLEAN THE OVEN
- SWEEP AND MOP THE FLOOR
-
-

LIVING ROOM:

- VACUUM THE COUCH
- VACUUM THE FLOOR
- WIPE SURFACES
- ARRANGE THE COUCH PILLOW
- CLEAN THE TV
- CHANGE THE CURTAINS
-
-

BATHROOM:

- CLEAN THE BATHTUB
- CLEAN THE TOILET
- CHANGE & WASH TOWELS
- REPLENISH TOILETRIES
- REFILL TOILET PAPER
- MOP THE FLOOR
-
-

BEDROOMS:

- CHANGE THE BED COVERS
- SWEEP & MOP THE FLOOR
- WASH THE LINENS
- ARRANGE THE DRESSER
- DUST PILLOWS
- CLEAN ALL THE SURFACES
-
-

OTHER:

-
-
-
-
-
-
-
-

OTHER:

-
-
-
-
-
-
-
-

ITEMS TO LET GO

SELL

DONATE

THROW AWAY

REPAIR OR REPLACE

REPAIR

REPLACE

NOTES

NOTES

30 DAY MONTHLY CHALLENGE

GOAL FOR THE MONTH:　　　　　J F M A M J J A S O N D

M	T	W	T	F	S	S

NOTES

MONTHLY PLAN

CHORES TO COMPLETE

WEEK BY WEEK

WEEK 1

WEEK 2

WEEK 3

WEEK 4

CLEANING CHECKLIST

KITCHEN:

- EMPTY THE DISHWASHER
- CLEAN ALL THE SURFACES
- TAKE OUT THE TRASH
- CLEAN THE REFRIGERATOR
- CLEAN THE OVEN
- SWEEP AND MOP THE FLOOR
-
-

LIVING ROOM:

- VACUUM THE COUCH
- VACUUM THE FLOOR
- WIPE SURFACES
- ARRANGE THE COUCH PILLOW
- CLEAN THE TV
- CHANGE THE CURTAINS
-
-

BATHROOM:

- CLEAN THE BATHTUB
- CLEAN THE TOILET
- CHANGE & WASH TOWELS
- REPLENISH TOILETRIES
- REFILL TOILET PAPER
- MOP THE FLOOR
-
-

BEDROOMS:

- CHANGE THE BED COVERS
- SWEEP & MOP THE FLOOR
- WASH THE LINENS
- ARRANGE THE DRESSER
- DUST PILLOWS
- CLEAN ALL THE SURFACES
-
-

OTHER:

-
-
-
-
-
-
-

OTHER:

-
-
-
-
-
-
-

ITEMS TO LET GO

SELL

DONATE

THROW AWAY

REPAIR OR REPLACE

REPAIR

REPLACE

NOTES

NOTES

30 DAY MONTHLY CHALLENGE

GOAL FOR THE MONTH: J F M A M J J A S O N D

M	T	W	T	F	S	S

NOTES

MONTHLY PLAN

CHORES TO COMPLETE

WEEK BY WEEK

WEEK 1

WEEK 2

WEEK 3

WEEK 4

CLEANING CHECKLIST

KITCHEN:

- EMPTY THE DISHWASHER
- CLEAN ALL THE SURFACES
- TAKE OUT THE TRASH
- CLEAN THE REFRIGERATOR
- CLEAN THE OVEN
- SWEEP AND MOP THE FLOOR
-
-

LIVING ROOM:

- VACUUM THE COUCH
- VACUUM THE FLOOR
- WIPE SURFACES
- ARRANGE THE COUCH PILLOW
- CLEAN THE TV
- CHANGE THE CURTAINS
-
-

BATHROOM:

- CLEAN THE BATHTUB
- CLEAN THE TOILET
- CHANGE & WASH TOWELS
- REPLENISH TOILETRIES
- REFILL TOILET PAPER
- MOP THE FLOOR
-
-

BEDROOMS:

- CHANGE THE BED COVERS
- SWEEP & MOP THE FLOOR
- WASH THE LINENS
- ARRANGE THE DRESSER
- DUST PILLOWS
- CLEAN ALL THE SURFACES
-
-

OTHER:

-
-
-
-
-
-
-

OTHER:

-
-
-
-
-
-
-

ITEMS TO LET GO

SELL

DONATE

THROW AWAY

REPAIR OR REPLACE

REPAIR

REPLACE

NOTES

NOTES

30 DAY MONTHLY CHALLENGE

GOAL FOR THE MONTH:　　　　　J F M A M J J A S O N D

M	T	W	T	F	S	S

NOTES

MONTHLY PLAN

CHORES TO COMPLETE

WEEK BY WEEK

WEEK 1

WEEK 2

WEEK 3

WEEK 4

CLEANING CHECKLIST

KITCHEN:
- EMPTY THE DISHWASHER
- CLEAN ALL THE SURFACES
- TAKE OUT THE TRASH
- CLEAN THE REFRIGERATOR
- CLEAN THE OVEN
- SWEEP AND MOP THE FLOOR

LIVING ROOM:
- VACUUM THE COUCH
- VACUUM THE FLOOR
- WIPE SURFACES
- ARRANGE THE COUCH PILLOW
- CLEAN THE TV
- CHANGE THE CURTAINS

BATHROOM:
- CLEAN THE BATHTUB
- CLEAN THE TOILET
- CHANGE & WASH TOWELS
- REPLENISH TOILETRIES
- REFILL TOILET PAPER
- MOP THE FLOOR

BEDROOMS:
- CHANGE THE BED COVERS
- SWEEP & MOP THE FLOOR
- WASH THE LINENS
- ARRANGE THE DRESSER
- DUST PILLOWS
- CLEAN ALL THE SURFACES

OTHER:

OTHER:

ITEMS TO LET GO

SELL

DONATE

THROW AWAY

REPAIR OR REPLACE

REPAIR

REPLACE

NOTES

NOTES

30 DAY MONTHLY CHALLENGE

GOAL FOR THE MONTH: J F M A M J J A S O N D

M	T	W	T	F	S	S

NOTES

MONTHLY PLAN

CHORES TO COMPLETE

WEEK BY WEEK

WEEK 1

WEEK 2

WEEK 3

WEEK 4

CLEANING CHECKLIST

KITCHEN:

- EMPTY THE DISHWASHER
- CLEAN ALL THE SURFACES
- TAKE OUT THE TRASH
- CLEAN THE REFRIGERATOR
- CLEAN THE OVEN
- SWEEP AND MOP THE FLOOR
-
-

LIVING ROOM:

- VACUUM THE COUCH
- VACUUM THE FLOOR
- WIPE SURFACES
- ARRANGE THE COUCH PILLOW
- CLEAN THE TV
- CHANGE THE CURTAINS
-
-

BATHROOM:

- CLEAN THE BATHTUB
- CLEAN THE TOILET
- CHANGE & WASH TOWELS
- REPLENISH TOILETRIES
- REFILL TOILET PAPER
- MOP THE FLOOR
-
-

BEDROOMS:

- CHANGE THE BED COVERS
- SWEEP & MOP THE FLOOR
- WASH THE LINENS
- ARRANGE THE DRESSER
- DUST PILLOWS
- CLEAN ALL THE SURFACES
-
-

OTHER:

-
-
-
-
-
-
-

OTHER:

-
-
-
-
-
-
-

ITEMS TO LET GO

SELL

DONATE

THROW AWAY

REPAIR OR REPLACE

REPAIR

REPLACE

NOTES

NOTES

30 DAY MONTHLY CHALLENGE

GOAL FOR THE MONTH:　　　　　　J F M A M J J A S O N D

M	T	W	T	F	S	S

NOTES

MONTHLY PLAN

CHORES TO COMPLETE

WEEK BY WEEK

WEEK 1

WEEK 2

WEEK 3

WEEK 4

CLEANING CHECKLIST

KITCHEN:

- EMPTY THE DISHWASHER
- CLEAN ALL THE SURFACES
- TAKE OUT THE TRASH
- CLEAN THE REFRIGERATOR
- CLEAN THE OVEN
- SWEEP AND MOP THE FLOOR

LIVING ROOM:

- VACUUM THE COUCH
- VACUUM THE FLOOR
- WIPE SURFACES
- ARRANGE THE COUCH PILLOW
- CLEAN THE TV
- CHANGE THE CURTAINS

BATHROOM:

- CLEAN THE BATHTUB
- CLEAN THE TOILET
- CHANGE & WASH TOWELS
- REPLENISH TOILETRIES
- REFILL TOILET PAPER
- MOP THE FLOOR

BEDROOMS:

- CHANGE THE BED COVERS
- SWEEP & MOP THE FLOOR
- WASH THE LINENS
- ARRANGE THE DRESSER
- DUST PILLOWS
- CLEAN ALL THE SURFACES

OTHER:

OTHER:

ITEMS TO LET GO

SELL

DONATE

THROW AWAY

REPAIR OR REPLACE

REPAIR

REPLACE

NOTES

NOTES

30 DAY MONTHLY CHALLENGE

GOAL FOR THE MONTH:　　　　J F M A M J J A S O N D

M	T	W	T	F	S	S

NOTES

MONTHLY PLAN

CHORES TO COMPLETE

WEEK BY WEEK

WEEK 1

WEEK 2

WEEK 3

WEEK 4

CLEANING CHECKLIST

KITCHEN:

- EMPTY THE DISHWASHER
- CLEAN ALL THE SURFACES
- TAKE OUT THE TRASH
- CLEAN THE REFRIGERATOR
- CLEAN THE OVEN
- SWEEP AND MOP THE FLOOR

LIVING ROOM:

- VACUUM THE COUCH
- VACUUM THE FLOOR
- WIPE SURFACES
- ARRANGE THE COUCH PILLOW
- CLEAN THE TV
- CHANGE THE CURTAINS

BATHROOM:

- CLEAN THE BATHTUB
- CLEAN THE TOILET
- CHANGE & WASH TOWELS
- REPLENISH TOILETRIES
- REFILL TOILET PAPER
- MOP THE FLOOR

BEDROOMS:

- CHANGE THE BED COVERS
- SWEEP & MOP THE FLOOR
- WASH THE LINENS
- ARRANGE THE DRESSER
- DUST PILLOWS
- CLEAN ALL THE SURFACES

OTHER:

OTHER:

ITEMS TO LET GO

SELL

DONATE

THROW AWAY

REPAIR OR REPLACE

REPAIR

REPLACE

NOTES

NOTES

30 DAY MONTHLY CHALLENGE

GOAL FOR THE MONTH: J F M A M J J A S O N D

M	T	W	T	F	S	S

NOTES

MONTHLY PLAN

CHORES TO COMPLETE

WEEK BY WEEK

WEEK 1

WEEK 2

WEEK 3

WEEK 4

CLEANING CHECKLIST

KITCHEN:
- EMPTY THE DISHWASHER
- CLEAN ALL THE SURFACES
- TAKE OUT THE TRASH
- CLEAN THE REFRIGERATOR
- CLEAN THE OVEN
- SWEEP AND MOP THE FLOOR
-
-

LIVING ROOM:
- VACUUM THE COUCH
- VACUUM THE FLOOR
- WIPE SURFACES
- ARRANGE THE COUCH PILLOW
- CLEAN THE TV
- CHANGE THE CURTAINS
-
-

BATHROOM:
- CLEAN THE BATHTUB
- CLEAN THE TOILET
- CHANGE & WASH TOWELS
- REPLENISH TOILETRIES
- REFILL TOILET PAPER
- MOP THE FLOOR
-
-

BEDROOMS:
- CHANGE THE BED COVERS
- SWEEP & MOP THE FLOOR
- WASH THE LINENS
- ARRANGE THE DRESSER
- DUST PILLOWS
- CLEAN ALL THE SURFACES
-
-

OTHER:
-
-
-
-
-
-
-

OTHER:
-
-
-
-
-
-
-

ITEMS TO LET GO

SELL

DONATE

THROW AWAY

REPAIR OR REPLACE

REPAIR

REPLACE

NOTES

NOTES

30 DAY MONTHLY CHALLENGE

GOAL FOR THE MONTH: J F M A M J J A S O N D

M	T	W	T	F	S	S

NOTES

MONTHLY PLAN

CHORES TO COMPLETE

WEEK BY WEEK

WEEK 1

WEEK 2

WEEK 3

WEEK 4

CLEANING CHECKLIST

KITCHEN:

- EMPTY THE DISHWASHER
- CLEAN ALL THE SURFACES
- TAKE OUT THE TRASH
- CLEAN THE REFRIGERATOR
- CLEAN THE OVEN
- SWEEP AND MOP THE FLOOR
-
-

LIVING ROOM:

- VACUUM THE COUCH
- VACUUM THE FLOOR
- WIPE SURFACES
- ARRANGE THE COUCH PILLOW
- CLEAN THE TV
- CHANGE THE CURTAINS
-
-

BATHROOM:

- CLEAN THE BATHTUB
- CLEAN THE TOILET
- CHANGE & WASH TOWELS
- REPLENISH TOILETRIES
- REFILL TOILET PAPER
- MOP THE FLOOR
-
-

BEDROOMS:

- CHANGE THE BED COVERS
- SWEEP & MOP THE FLOOR
- WASH THE LINENS
- ARRANGE THE DRESSER
- DUST PILLOWS
- CLEAN ALL THE SURFACES
-
-

OTHER:

-
-
-
-
-
-
-

OTHER:

-
-
-
-
-
-
-

ITEMS TO LET GO

SELL

DONATE

THROW AWAY

REPAIR OR REPLACE

REPAIR

REPLACE

NOTES

NOTES

NOTES

NOTES

NOTES

NOTES

NOTES

NOTES

NOTES

NOTES

NOTES

Printed in Great Britain
by Amazon